A SIMPLE GUIDE TO
THE HISTORY AND MEANING OF
THE PSALMS

A SIMPLE GUIDE TO
THE HISTORY AND MEANING OF

THE PSALMS

By
Canon Dudley Hodges

SALISBURY
1993

© **Copyright 1993**: Canon Dudley Hodges
ISBN 0-9521795-0-4
Published by Adept Services
Type layout: JHC Communication, Salisbury.
Printed by Jill Bullen, Alvediston, Nr. Salisbury.
Acknowledgements:
The author acknowledges with gratitude, the help received from
Roslyn Chillingworth, Suzanne Eward and Walter Partridge.

THE PSALMS

FOREWORD

Canon Hodges' beautifully clear and spiritually sympathetic Guide to the Psalms will, I am sure, be of great help to those who, either in private or in church, follow the Offices of the Church of England in their Daily prayers.

Others too will find here just the informed and relevant guidance they need to make the Psalms come alive for Christian devotion.

It is a great pleasure to be allowed to commend this work of a priest and man of prayer for whom, along with many hundreds of others, I have the most grateful love and admiration. I pray that it will be richly blessed to many.

Easter 1993
✝ **John Sarum**

THE AUTHOR

Throughout his Ministry, Canon Dudley Hodges, M.A. has been dedicated to the pastoral needs of his parishioners.

Now, Canon Emeritus of Salisbury Cathedral, he studied for the Ministry at Cuddesdon Theological College. Ordained in 1932, he joined the staff of Southwark Cathedral as Deacon, he became Vicar of the Church of the Holy Spirit, Clapham, South West London in 1939. With his wife, Margery, he moved first to Eltham, Kent and then to the Midlands, where for ten years he was Rector and Rural Dean of Stafford.

For another decade, he carried heavy responsibility as Canon Residentiary and Precentor of Lichfield Cathedral, with additional duties as Director of Ordinands. Retiring in 1976, to live in The Cathedral Close in Salisbury, he was soon a natural choice to become Vicar of the Close, a post he held for eight years. All those who have known him in his retiring years will tell you, his pastoral care was deeply appreciated by his flock in The Close and beyond.

He knew every one by name, as a good shepherd should, and it is to the many seekers after Christian knowledge he has known, indeed to all those whose Faith is enriched by the Offices of the Church of England, he dedicates this slender volume.

J.H.C

****

THE PSALMS
CONTENTS

	Page No.
Foreword...	*v*
Preface..	*ix*
Introduction...	*xiii*
DAY ONE..	3 - 4
DAY TWO..	5 - 6
DAY THREE..	7 - 8
DAY FOUR..	9 - 10
DAY FIVE..	11 - 12
DAY SIX..	13
DAY SEVEN..	14 - 15
DAY EIGHT..	15 - 17
DAY NINE...	17 - 19
DAY TEN...	19 - 21
DAY ELEVEN...	22 - 23
DAY TWELVE..	24 - 25
DAY THIRTEEN...	25 - 26
DAY FOURTEEN...	27
DAY FIFTEEN..	28 - 29
DAY SIXTEEN..	30 - 31
DAY SEVENTEEN..	32 - 33
DAY EIGHTEEN...	33 - 35
DAY NINETEEN...	35 - 36
DAY TWENTY..	37 - 38
DAY TWENTY-ONE...	38 - 39
DAY TWENTY-TWO..	39 - 40
DAY TWENTY-THREE..	41 - 42
DAY TWENTY-FOUR......................Morning	42
DAY TWENTY-FOUR, TWENTY-FIVE, TWENTY-SIX . . Evening	43
DAY TWENTY-FIVE AND TWENTY-SIX.............Morning	43
DAY TWENTY-SEVEN...	43 - 45
DAY TWENTY-EIGHT...	46 - 47
DAY TWENTY-NINE...	48 - 49
DAY THIRTY...	49 - 51
THE PSALMS - Some Key Quotations..................	52 - 53

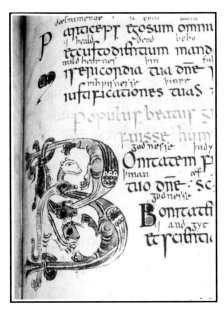

Psalm 119, verse 65
"Bonitatem fecisti cum servo tuo, Domine, secundum tuum".
"O Lord, thou hast dealt graciously with thy servant:
according unto thy word".

PREFACE

The purpose of this simple booklet on the psalms is the hope that help may be given to the reader through knowing a little more of the time and the circumstances in which the psalms were written. It is hoped that perhaps those who appreciate the daily choral Evensong may be able to find spiritual meaning coming out all the more clearly through the historical treatment.

There is nothing original as far as the scholarship is concerned; all the information contained is the result of some research into other peoples' work. It is impossible to discover the exact time and occasion of every psalm, yet there are few of which we cannot be sure to what group they belong, or the general period and occasion with reasonable certainty.

It is a humble attempt to restore the Psalter as far as possible to the order in which the psalms were written, by dividing them up into five distinct historical groups.

Period 1

The Psalms of David and of his time

David is rightly styled as not only the founder of the Hebrew monarchy but of the Hebrew Psalter. As God raised up Moses to give to his people and to his church a rule of law, so he raised up David as King and to be the sweet singer of his Israel. Of this King and Psalmist we know from the history of his life that he had a great gift of leadership and faith in Jehovah.
     No King but David had such a sense of his own majesty and of the fact that he had been set apart by God's grace and raised up above all men, (i.e. Psalm 101.) He also had a great love of nature from his shepherd's life which we can see in Psalms 8, 19, 29 and in the 23rd Psalm.

Period 2

Psalms of the Monarchy from David to the Captivity

When we pass through the age of David we pass from growth to decadence. The whole period from David to Hezekiah is one of degeneracy and decay. Some attempts were made to reform the Kingdom but it is probable that the northern tribes deserted the Temple for the more attractive worship of the high places, paying little honour to the material temple. How could they then maintain the spiritual temple of which David laid the foundation? Where is now in this period the national enthusiasm and devotional spirit?

Period 3

Psalms from the destruction of the Kingdom to the return from Captivity

Some of the grandest and most spiritual psalms are the outcome of the Captivity in spite of the humiliation, and there are flashes of the noblest thought. It seems as if the very separation from their beloved land and the security of the temple worship could alone open the eyes of Hebrew people to the truth that spiritual life and happiness is in God. In their deep distress they recognise the greatness of their sin and forgetfulness of God himself.

Therefore hope and trust are not quenched but purified and strengthened. The old Israel rises again to new life from its distress and sorrow.

Period 4

Psalms from the period of the re-building of Jerusalem.

Nations do not usually survive dispersion. As long as they retain their country they may survive conquest, but while Israel melted away in Assyria, Judah alone proved indestructible. With great faith in the future the inspired statesmen of Judah accepted the loss of country and home as necessary for recovery of true religion. Jeremiah in his prophecy seems to have given up all thought for national independence and to have welcomed the sharp remedy of captivity and dispersion as the only cure for the growing evil of national corruption.

Judah was purified by adversity but other lessons should have been learnt of a more merciful approach to other nations and peoples. However national corruption was stayed and within about 70 years Judah had recovered its country. Some of the lessons the people had learnt were the power of repentance; acknowledging the imperfection of the past; the value of prayer and the evil and vanity of idols. Having brought the nation's belief in Jehovah into contempt they must now re-establish it by a restoration of Jerusalem and the conversion of all the nations of the world.

Period 5

The Close of the Psalter.

We have arrived at a period towards the end of the 5th and beginning of the 4th century before the Christian era, when the prophets and upholders of the spiritual life of the Hebrew nation had passed away. In this situation there is no longer the inspiration of psalmody. They are mainly psalms of personal experience in this period but they are still equal to the old models in depth of thought and beauty of expression.

Never did real religion burn with a brighter light as the struggle with the world had ceased and there were no fiery trials so that there is a fervour and a glow which seems to burn in the heart of each member of the congregation. They seem to have acquired the abiding spiritual life which no outward disasters can take away. This period closes with grand congregational psalms for the little remnant of the new Jerusalem.

A SIMPLE GUIDE TO THE HISTORY AND MEANING OF THE PSALMS

INTRODUCTION

The psalms themselves are a collection of prayers, meditations and songs first put together for the return of the Jews from exile, though many of them were in regular use long before this. They were used in the worship of the Temple or written as personal prayers that were later adopted for use by the whole community.

The psalms went on to play a central part in the worship of the synagogue and home and were inherited by the early Christians, remaining in constant use for both public and private worship ever since. The psalms express the religious ideas and belief of Israel as the chosen people of God, together with the hopes and ideals of the times when they were written. They belong to different ages and reveal signs of spiritual development.

Ideas of God

The idea of God which comes through the psalms is, necessarily, inferior to the Christian's. We should not confuse the picture of God in the psalms with that believed in by Jews today, which has of course also developed greatly. He is a majestic individual, all-powerful, just, and compassionate to His people. However there is no thought of His nearness nor of the New Testament "We may dwell in Him and He in us", with all that means.

He is the Creator and Sustainer of life. He judges and punishes all who disobey Him whether His own people or those of other nations. His loved ones who obey Him, He will protect, rescue and avenge. God dwells in the heavens "among the clouds". He "comes" or "sends down from on high" to help His people but at the same time He is present on earth in the Temple in Jerusalem.

We believe that the Jewish people were chosen by God because they were an outstandingly religious nation. God has always been the same but He moved among the prophets and psalmists of the Old Testament so that His people might gradually come to know Him better, for what He really is and comprehend His goodness, love, justice and mercy.

Universalism

The existence of others gods is accepted for other nations. (Psalm 81 vv. 9 and 10). "There shall be no strange god among you". However, after the exile, passages about the idols of the nations in Psalm 115 vv. 4 - 8 and Psalm 135 vv. 15-18 clearly do reflect a belief in absolute monotheism, that Jehovah is the God of the whole earth. Even when the existence of other gods is not denied in the psalms, it is the superiority of Jehovah (Yahweh) e.g. Psalm 95 v. 3 "For the Lord is a great God and great King above all gods" or Psalm 97 v. 9 " ... thou art exalted far above all gods".

The greatness of God

The Psalmists were united in their thoughts of God's greatness, glory, and loving kindness. Nothing can be found anywhere to compare with the depth and beauty of their praise. The Hebrew title of the Psalter can be translated as "Praises", and they were sung with great fervour in the Temple courts. The reason for the continual praising of Jehovah in the psalms is His constant attitude of mercy, loyalty and loving kindness towards the Israelites both collectively and individually. Psalms 17 and 136 are good examples.

Some practical points

The psalms may be described as Hebrew poetry and follow the pattern of what is called parallelism or "double blow of the hammer" or couplets.

The second part after the colon of each verse most often reiterates or amplifies the first. For examples Psalm 29 v.7, Psalm 34 v.7, Psalm 73 v.15, and Psalm 145 v.13. This is why it is important not to rush through the psalms but to take notice of the colon and have at least one or two beats - otherwise the rhythm is spoilt.

When Matins or Evensong is said, the congregation must not give way to the general rush - not a long pause at the colon but at least a breath or one beat, and then the psalms will be said as they should be.

When saying the psalms like this, it is important for each individual to speak only loud enough, to be able to hear the words spoken by their immediate neighbour. This is why the choir at sung Evensong sing the psalms antiphonally.

The decani side sing the first part of the verse and then the cantoris side sing the second half. In so doing the characteristic of the Hebrew poetry is emphasised. The psalms are Christianised by the choir singing the Gloria which is important and justifies the incorporation of the psalms into Christian worship.

It is important to notice the different changes of chant in the longer psalms to express the Psalmist's moods and depths of feeling.

Also the organ accompaniment to the psalms is not just what may come into the Organist's mind at the time but by concentrating on the verses he assists in bringing out the full meaning of the words through his playing, and this helps the listener to use his or her imagination in worship.

Attitude towards enemies.

It is very difficult sometimes to understand the attitude of the Psalmists towards their enemies. We have to remember that the Hebrew people were a tiny nation in the midst of hostile races and they believed that their nation, Israel, had been selected by God to be His own chosen people and to be taught His commandments.

The Psalmist could say " In the name of the Lord will I destroy the enemy" and he could pray in the fiercest pre-Christian language that God would exterminate their enemies. This was not so much in the spirit of vengeance for themselves, but for the desire to vindicate God's own honour. God's own righteousness, dignity and honour could not be vindicated until He had "rewarded the proud after their deserving".

We need also, to understand more fully the experience of intense suffering which the people had in an alien country during the exile. Also that judgement of the wicked had to happen in this world (just as the righteous had to be rewarded) because there was little belief in an after-life.

The problem was that if their belief in themselves as the chosen people of God was correct then how could He allow them to suffer when they had been true to Him and their enemies had not? Suffering in those times was always regarded as a punishment for sin.

Therefore, the Israelites were able to cling to the certainty that somehow the wicked would be punished and the righteous rewarded. This explains the apparent self-righteousness of the Psalmists which appears so often.

Christians, of course, cannot make the language of vindictiveness their own. For Christ taught us to love our enemies (that is, that we must always be ready to do them good should it be necessary) and this is why, rightly or wrongly, some passages of the psalms which proclaim the slaughter and destruction of Israel's enemies are excluded when they are set to be said or sung.

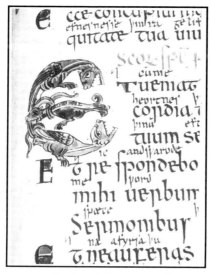

Psalm 119, verse 41
"Et veniat super me misericordia tua, Domine".
"Let thy loving mercy come also unto me, O Lord".

◆

The Salisbury Psalter

Salisbury Cathedral Library Manuscript 150

The illustrations in this book are taken from the famous Psalter that belongs to Salisbury Cathedral Library, and are reproduced by kind permission of the Dean and Chapter.

Written on vellum in c. 970 AD, it is a Latin Psalter of the Gallican version, with interlinear translations in Anglo-Saxon added c. 1100.

Each psalm begins with a beautifully decorated initial letter, chiefly formed of dragons, beasts and birds. The treasured volume is thought to have been written for the Benedictine nunnery of Wilton, and may possibly have belonged to St Edith, 960 - 984. Expert opinion places it amongst the earliest surviving Gallican Psalters written in England.

Suzanne Eward
Librarian and Keeper of the Muniments
Salisbury Cathedral

Bless the Lord, O my soul,
And all that is within me
Bless His holy name.
Bless the Lord, O my soul,
And forget not all his benefits.....

Psalm 103

THE PSALMS

The Prayer book version of the Psalter of 1662, attributed to Coverdale, lasted without any kind of revision until 1958 when the Revised Psalter was produced by the Archbishops' commission and introduced to Salisbury Cathedral by Canon Cyril Taylor, the precentor at that time.

With the coming of Series Three, now known as Rite A, by the Church of England Liturgical commission, a truly modern Psalter but still basically a revision of Coverdale was incorporated into the Alternative Service Book 1980. Psalms are used in Christian worship, not simply as records of Jewish history, but because their history is typical of the Catholic Church throughout the ages - privileged, sinning, forgiven, renewed.

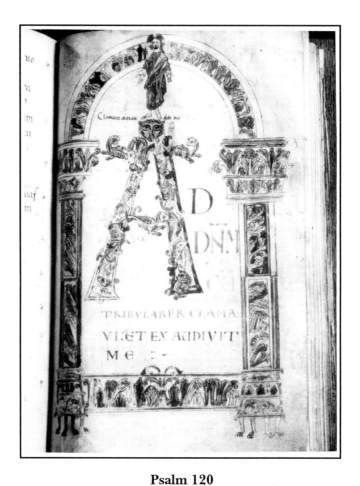

Psalm 120
"Ad Dominum, cum tribularer, clamavi: et exaudivit me".
"When I was in trouble I called upon the Lord:
and he heard me".

DAY ONE

Morning Prayer

Psalm 1. This psalm strikes the key note, as it were, of the whole Psalter and it might easily have been written to stand at the head of all the psalms to indicate the train of thought in which they should be read. It illustrates the faithfulness of God's dealing with man and indicates the difference between those who have a religious duty and those who have not. Period 2.

Psalm 2. This psalm is from Period 1 and seems to come from the time of the coronation of Solomon as King as it breathes the calmness of power and inspiration when the nation is menaced by disruptions. After David's time, of course, other near nations soon broke out in rebellion against Israel.

vv. 1 - 3 The Psalmist wonders at the conspiracy of the rebellious nations.
vv. 4 - 6 God hears and replies.
vv. 7 - 9 The King reminds the people of the words spoken at his coronation.
vv. 10 -12 Advises loyalty to Jehovah.

Psalm 3. Also from Period 1 and probably written by David in an hour of peril, and seems to express his feeling in the time of Absalom's rebellion. It is marked by the sense of communion with God and calm confidence in His protection; with the tender love which even forbids him to mention his son's name.

vv. 1 - 2 In the hours of despair....
vv. 3 - 4 recollects former favours of God..
vv. 5 - end Faith renewed by sleep and prays for his people.

Psalm 4. Also from Period 1. A real Even-song and belongs to the time of the last psalm. The royal dignity of David's character comes from his sense of the covenant between God and himself as the anointed King. The absence of any desire for revenge is very striking when we remember the feelings of the age in which the psalms were written.

vv. 1 - 5   Psalmist appeals to God and urges his slanderers to repent.

vv. 6 - 9   He prays for help to cheer his friends for he himself does trust in God.

Psalm 5. From Period 2 and designed for the service of the Temple. The Psalmist feels that as he offers his morning worship, he is proclaiming his belief in Jehovah and any unworthiness that may follow will not only disgrace himself but will allow enemies of Jehovah to sneer at the frailty of His worshippers. How applicable today when we give opportunity to those who scorn religion because of our own weaknesses.

vv. 1 - 6   The Psalmist appeals to God to hear him because he knows that God always helps the godly.

vv. 7 - end   God always defeats the plots of the wicked.

DAY ONE

Evening Prayer

Psalm 6. This comes from the second Period of psalms after the age of growth with David and decadence after his death. This is a prayer for deliverance from sickness.

vv. 4 & 5   Before it is too late and ....

vv. 8 - 10   assurance that prayer is answered.

Psalm 7. This psalm is earlier than the previous one and comes from the time of David - Period 1, and relates to the establishment of the Kingdom in spite of strong resistance from the enemies of Israel. Of this King David we know that he had great faith in Jehovah or Yahweh (the more accurate representation of Old Testament name for God) and the psalm was undoubtedly written by him.

vv. 1 - 5   David pleads that his hands are free from treachery and ...
vv. 6 - 12 trusts his cause to God.
vv. 13 - 18 God will make the plots of traitors recoil on themselves.

Psalm 8. This psalm is also from David's time - Period 1. The Hebrews were distinguished by one great characteristic, their belief in the Unseen; (marked by their lyrical poetry). The great spiritual truth that God made man in His own image flashes forth in this psalm (e.g. Genesis Chapter 1 v. 26). David in his shepherd life brought him into communion with God and His creation.

vv. 1 & 2 Testimony of infancy to the Glory of God.
vv. 3 - 8 The physical weakness and spiritual dignity of man.

DAY TWO

Morning Prayer

Psalm 9 and 10. Both come from Period 2 and were composed for the Temple worship. As Jerusalem was still not destroyed these two psalms form a thanksgiving for proof of divine vengeance, on one or other of the other great empires of the times.

Psalm 10
vv. 1 - 12   This is a more detailed description of those troubles
vv. 13 - end Renewed prayer to Jehovah to bring a final deliverance from them.
Psalm 11. This psalm is from Period 1, and must have come from the earlier days of David when he had to maintain his struggle against the constant jealousy of Saul. David's friends had cowardly fears and were in despair for him. David still has a great trust in God and pours forth in this psalm his firm and simple faith.
vv. 1 - 7   Psalmist's answer to the despair of his friends and he is comforted by his conviction of the justice of God.
v. 8   Shows that David believes God cares for the righteous.

DAY TWO

Evening Prayer

Psalm 12. With Psalm 13 these two psalms are probably from Period 2; that is from the end of the monarchy of David to the Captivity. The whole period from David to Hezekiah was one of degeneracy and decay. In Psalm 12 the Psalmist is appalled by the rottenness of society around him, unscrupulous ambition appears to rule supreme, and truth is scorned as folly. But God has not left himself without a witness; prophets had already raised their voices against this corruption.
vv. 1 & 2   The help of God is needed against the untruth...
vv. 3 & 4   and against the pride of the oppressors.
vv. 5 & 6   The Psalmist thinks of the words of the prophets..
vv. 7 & 8   and feels assured of God's protection.

Psalm 13. Period 2. The struggles for the faithful people of Israel are not so much in this period against heathen enemies, but against the godless among their own people. Hence these psalms are mostly personal; sickness may cut short the Psalmist's career of service to God.

vv. 1 & 2   Appeals to God for deliverance from sickness ...
vv. 3 & 4   before it is too late.
vv. 5 & 6   Trusts that his prayer will be answered.

Psalm 14. (Psalm 53 is a different version). This psalm is from the Third Period, the destruction of the Kingdom to the beginning of the return from Captivity. Hope and trust are not quenched but strengthened in spite of peoples' humiliation.

vv. 1 - 3   God sees the corruption of the nations...
vv. 4 - 8   and rebukes it from heaven.
vv. 9 - 10 The heathen are confounded by God.
v. 11   Prayer for the restitution of Israel.

DAY THREE

Morning Prayer

Psalm 15. This comes from Period 1 and we learn that the Ark at Jerusalem was the centre of national worship, but for David the symbol of the presence of God could not be placed above the truth which it signified. This psalm has great value for every age in keeping before the mind the great lesson that holiness of life and truth of heart are the absolute essentials for spiritual religion.

Psalm 16. Period 3. This psalm along with Psalms 17 and 49 show the first signs of belief that there is life for the soul with God when flesh and worldly glory perish. All trace of struggle and fear is gone and the psalm is full of hope and the sunshine of peace and joy.

vv. 1 - 9 The Psalmist has great confidence in Jehovah, joy in His presence which is a strength against temptation.
vv.10 - end Reminds the Psalmist that in God's presence is everlasting life.

Psalm 17. This is from Period 3 once more and was possibly written in the midst of persecution, either from a tyrant, or from heathen or from idolatrous Israelites. The psalm is full of hope and despair alternatively. We read here the thoughts of one who has to face the great problem of the time when the wicked prospered.
vv. 1 - 6 The Psalmist praises God in the confidence of his own honesty.
vv. 7 - 12 Prays against the persecution of the wicked.
vv. 13 - end Though the wicked prosper the Psalmist may have the blessing of the holy God's presence.

DAY THREE

Evening Prayer

Psalm 18. This is the longest and noblest of David's psalms and comes from Period 1, composed during the last years of his prosperous life.
vv. 1 & 2 David praises God his deliverer...
vv. 3 - 19 who has rescued him from all the perils of his life.
vv. 20 - 30 According to the character of everyone so does God reveal Himself to them.
vv. 31 - 46 God has given David strength to subdues his enemies and make the nations pay tribute to him.
vv. 47 - 51 David returns to the praise of God his deliverer.

DAY FOUR

Morning Prayer

Psalm 19. From Period 1. The calm bright sky which sheds its splendour every day over Palestine moves the Poet to write the first part of this psalm. He sees God revealed in nature (David as the possible author), and in the second half of the psalm, which may have been written much later by someone else, concentrates on the revelation of God in the Jewish Law.

vv. 1 - 6   The Glory of God in creation.
vv. 7 - end The Glory of God in his Law.

Psalm 20. From Period 2. An antiphonal hymn sung alternatively by congregation and priest in the Temple before a struggle against the enemies of Israel. They believed that right is might and that God can save in spite of a great host arrayed against them.

vv. 1 - 5   The people pray for the success of the King in full assurance of victory.
vv. 6 - 8   The Priest confirms the triumph of their faith and the last verse is sung by the people.

Psalm 21. Also from Period 2. In this psalm the prophet feels that it is part of his duty to remind the people of the necessity of loyalty to the King (most likely Solomon) and by so doing honouring Jehovah himself who anointed him. The occasion of the psalm is some celebration, such as the King's Birthday or Accession and is a hymn for priest and people.

vv. 1 - 7   The peoples' part.
vv. 8 - 12   The Priest's part addressing the King.
v. 13   The peoples' response.

DAY FOUR
Evening Prayer

Psalm 22. The Psalmist is apparently in exile and in the hands of his captors. His extreme peril, and imminent death are touched on with a tenderness and power which have made the language familiar to us in the Passion and death of Christ. (This psalm is always used on Good Friday).

vv. 1 - 11 Psalmist cries to God but is forsaken and mocked, yet he prays to his Helper of old.

vv. 12 - 18 Enemies surround him in his suffering and condemnation.

vv. 19 - 21 Yet he renews his prayer.

vv. 22 - 28 On his delivery, he will cause God to be praised by all the world.

vv. 29 - 32 His story will comfort the suffering and live for ever.

Psalm 23. Period 2. Whatever may have been the occasion of this psalm there is but one recorded life with which we can associate it - the royal shepherd David on the lonely hillsides of Judah when he was learning the secret of inner strength. David who had come to look back on his kingdom in old age, not as a prize which he had won but as a trust committed to him, remembering that the Lord was his shepherd, the shepherd of every Israelite.

vv. 1 - 3 Loving care of God.

vv. 4 - 6 A dark valley, gloomy as death, yet God entertains the traveller in defiance of his pursuers. What a comfort this psalm has been to so many.

DAY FIVE

Morning Prayer

Psalm 24. Period 1. Triumphal entry of the Ark into the City, establishing David's kingdom, is commemorated in this psalm. David and the deep religious feeling of the nation bring a new revelation of the majesty of Jehovah.

vv. 1 - 3 God is the Creator of the World therefore who can come into His presence?
vv. 4 - 6 The answer.
v. 7 Choir of Priests approaching the gates of Jerusalem.
v. 8 Warders from within followed by priests' answer.
v. 9 Repeated request from the priests.
v. 10 Wardens and Priests answer one another once more.

Psalm 25 From Period 3. This psalm is a declaration of God's goodness to the holy and a prayer for growth in good living, and probably has the same author as Psalm 34.

Psalm 26. From Period 2. A psalm composed apparently for a time of sickness or a plague which has descended on the author. Such sickness was regarded as a punishment for some sin or national apostasy.

vv. 1 - 7 The Psalmist testifies to his honesty.
vv. 8 - 10 Claims deliverance from the affliction.
vv. 11 & 12 He abides in hope.

DAY FIVE

Evening Prayer

Psalm 27. Period 2. The first part of this psalm recalls the triumph of a warrior's faith.
vv. 1 - 3 What terrors have the perils of war for a man who has found his protection in the help of the Almighty?
vv. 4 - 7 Second part of this psalm is a prayer of a priest or a prophet. Not in peril on the battlefield but exposed to persecutors and despair, very different from the first part of hope and confidence.
vv. 8 - 14 A plaintive cry to God to be with him in his need and probably written at the close of the monarchy at the time of religious persecution.
vv. 15 & 16 Return to the belief that God is the only safety in peril.

Psalm 28. This one is also from Period 2, composed probably by a King, written under circumstances of urgent danger.
vv. 1 - 6 The Psalmist's prayer for deliverance.
vv. 7 - 10 The deliverance is granted and he returns thanks. These last verses may have been added later when the afflictions described in the earlier verses were over.

Psalm 29. There is nothing in all creation which brings home to the Hebrews the omnipotence of God and influence of heaven upon earth more than a thunder storm. This psalm comes from Period 1.
vv. 1 - 8 This psalm calls for the worship of God when He reveals Himself in thunder and lightning to the world.
vv. 9 & 10 Although God is a King above the mighty flood He will give His people strength and the blessing of peace.

DAY SIX
Morning Prayer

Psalm 30. From Period 2. In the calm after the storm the Psalmist sees the working of God's ways in the illness which had afflicted him and in all that has perplexed him as far as his faith was concerned.
vv. 1 - 5 The Psalmist praises God for deliverance and encourages others to do the same.
vv. 6 - end He tells how his self confidence was rebuked but his prayer for life accepted.

Psalm 31. Also from Period 2. The Psalmist is persecuted for his faithfulness to Jehovah. It may have been Jeremiah who was the author as his cry goes up in similar words and mood to those in his prophetic book.
vv. 1 - 7 The Psalmist declares his confidence in God.
vv. 8 - 14 He asks for help in sorrow and suffering.
vv. 15 - 20 Declares once more his confidence in Jehovah.
vv. 21 - end Rejoicing once more in the fulfilment of his prayer.

DAY SIX
Evening Prayer

Psalm 32. This psalm comes from the First Period of David's time, undoubtedly written by him and the occasion is to be sought in the history of Bathsheba. From its penitential character David has learnt to live in communion with God and that there is no happiness for man without openness before God.
vv. 1 & 2 The Psalmist declares the blessing of openness before God.
vv. 3 - 6 Quotes his own experience of sin.
vv. 7 - 9 Exhorts all to turn to God.
vv. 10 - 12 And not to withstand Him.

Psalm 33. This comes from the Fifth Period of psalms (end of 5th and beginning of the 4th Century before the Christian era) and is designed for a public festival to celebrate deliverance from some powerful heathen nation.
vv. 1 - 3   Call to praise God.
vv. 4 - 11   Because He is the God who made and keeps the Universe ...
vv. 12 - 21   He has blest His people Israel.

Psalm 34. This psalm comes from the Third Period of the Psalter History - from the destruction of the Kingdom of Israel to the return from the peoples' captivity in Assyria. Agony and ordeal of their separation from their beloved land does not quench their hope and trust in God.
vv. 1 - 22   This whole psalm is an exhortation to praise God for His mercies in spite of the humiliation they are suffering in exile.

DAY SEVEN
Morning Prayer

Psalm 35. From Period 3. In this psalm the author appears to have been persecuted by hostile enemies who have brought false charges against him and to have contracted a dangerous illness, which only God can change and heal on his behalf.
vv. 1 - 10   The Psalmist prays to God to do battle against his enemies.
vv. 11 - 19   He justifies his prayer by describing the deceit and ingratitude of his enemies.
vv. 20 - end   He pleads his righteousness for God to act on his behalf.

Psalm 36. From Period 2. A condemnation of those who are deliberately hostile to what is right and whose consciences have been silenced.

vv. 1 - 4 The ungodly rejoice in their misdeeds.
vv. 5 - 8 But God is just who will protect His own ....
vv. 9 - 12 ... and overthrow the wicked.

DAY SEVEN
Evening Prayer

Psalm 37. This comes from Period 2 of the psalms. The connection between wickedness and punishment was a lesson impressed on the people of this time and age by the destruction of unrighteous empires and tyrants. The Psalmist urges the people not to envy the present prosperity of the wicked because they will be destroyed in the end.
vv. 1 - 11 The righteous are exalted to disregard the prosperity of the wicked.
vv. 12 - 20 Their wickedness is but for a time.
vv. 21 - 41 While the righteous have the abiding protection of God.

DAY EIGHT
Morning Prayer

Psalm 38. The Psalmist appears to have met with powerful persecutors and in the hour of his weakness they glory in his misfortunes, both his enemies and those he has befriended. From Period 3.
vv. 1 - 8 The Psalmist in his sickness prays for the relief of his punishment....
vv. 9 - 15 and calls on God to witness his patience in pain, desertion and danger.
vv. 16 - 22 And finally prays for help; for his fall would allow the enemies of God to rejoice.

Psalm 39. Period 2. One of the most beautiful of lamentations in the Psalter. The struggle here is not against the wicked or godless but against death itself. To the Psalmist the approach of death would have been appalling anyhow but doubly bitter when the ungodly and the scoffer look upon his afflictions as a sign that God has deserted him. His pain must be endured in silence, yet in hope and in prayer the Psalmist finds comfort but this is still short of the Christian's highest hope of victory over death.

vv. 1 - 7 The Psalmist would like to keep silent before the wicked but pain compels him to speak.

vv. 8 -12 Amid his misery he finds help in God.

vv.13 - end He seeks rest in an appeal to God's compassion.

Psalm 40. Period 3. (Compare Psalm 70) This psalm really consists of two parts and instead of the usual order in which a prayer comes first followed by thanksgiving and praise, we have here first thanksgiving for deliverance and then a prayer for help. Affliction has brought him nearer to God and given him a deeper understanding of His will.

vv. 1 - 7 The Psalmist facing peril is reminded of a previous deliverance from a similar situation.

vv. 8 - 13 This recollection fills him with hope and lifts him from his despair. Jehovah is not merely a God of vengeance but of righteousness.

vv.14 - end A renewed appeal for God's help.

DAY EIGHT
Evening Prayer

Psalm 41. This psalm comes from the period and group of psalms during the monarchy from David to the Captivity of the Hebrews.
vv. 1 - 3   Blessing received from sympathy for the suffering.
vv. 4 - 6   When the Psalmist appeals to God against the treacherous cruelty of his enemies....
vv. 7 - 9   and their joy at his suffering....
vv. 10 - end   His prayer is heard.

Psalm 42. This psalm is from the Period 3.
vv. 1 - 7   The Psalmist dwells lovingly on the joyous festivals of the Temple.
vv. 8 - 15   Takes last look at his own land and is overwhelmed with grief.

Psalm 43. This is part of Psalm 42.
vv. 1 - 6   This psalm rises to hope in the thought that God in His justice would restore the writer to Jerusalem.

DAY NINE
Morning Prayer

Psalm 44. Psalm 44 written during Period 4. This is one of the psalms which express anguish and perplexity which follows the return of the Jews from Captivity. Expectations were high for the arrival of that glorious time when the Israelites should dwell in the city of David and the walls of the city would be rebuilt, and the citizens united. However the expected blessing did not come and there was some calamity, the source of which is uncertain.
vv. 1 - 9   The Psalmist resorts to memory of God's former blessings.

vv.10 - 17   He complains of the present evils.
vv. 18 - end Although desolation reigns not only in the land but in the holy city, the Psalmist states the faithfulness of the nation and cries unto God for his help.

Psalm 45. From Period 2. The special occasion for this psalm seems to be the entrance of a bride in procession into the palace of the royal bridegroom. The spiritual insight of this psalm is that it is not just the perfection of the King's justice, his personal beauty or victory in battles, but that these attributes are all the blessings of God. The King is in union with the Divine Ruler.

vv.   1 - 3   The Psalmist speaks of the King's beauty and gracious presence as proofs of God's favour.
vv.   4 - 8   The King is promised success as a warrior because of his justice.
vv. 9 - 13   The Queen approaches.
vv. 14 -18   The Queen enters in all her beauty.

Psalm 46. From Period 2. Few events in the history of Israel influenced the national character more than the repulse of the Assyrian invasion because it was reckoned as a proof of divine deliverance from oppression. There became increased reverence for the Holy City and the Temple. The golden age of Moses and David seemed to return. Also the belief was here beginning to emerge that their religion was to triumph not by extermination of their opponents but by winning them over to the allegiance of Jehovah.

vv.   1 - 3   God as a refuge in storm and tempest.
vv.   4 - 7   God's presence given to the besieged.
vv. 8 to end His great deliverance in destroying the Assyrians.

DAY NINE
Evening Prayer

Psalm 47. Psalm composed for the dedication of the Temple and sung during the processions. This psalm comes from Period 4.
vv. 1 - 4   An invitation to all lands to praise the Lord.
vv. 5 - 8   God whose earthly throne is the Hill of Zion.
v. 9   Rulers do Him homage, for He is the King of Kings.

Psalm 48. This psalm was mainly designed as a temple song and before the degeneracy had taken place. Period 2.
vv. 1 - 2   The beauty of Zion, the dwelling of God.
vv. 3 - 7   Terror of the allied kings at the sight of the city of Jerusalem.
vv. 8 - 13   Judah celebrates God's loving kindness in the Temple. The Assyrians had threatened the capture of Zion. (Compare Chapter 33 of Isaiah).

Psalm 49. A summons to hear the great lesson that there is really nothing to fear. This psalm comes from Period 3.
vv. 1 - 12   The prosperity of the wicked need cause no anxiety; for wealth without God is of no avail.
vv. 13 - 20   Death is the end of the foolish but the righteous have length of days.

DAY TEN
Morning Prayer

Psalm 50. From Period 2. The Psalmist sees the Almighty as the object of great superstitious reverence, misguided worship and lack of a real spiritual religion. The outward worship of Jehovah had been established but it was followed by formalism and hypocrisy.

vv.   1 - 6 A description of God's forthcoming judgement.
vv.   7 - 15 God passes sentence on the nation .....
vv. 16 - 21 and especially on the wicked.
vv. 22 & 23 His words of mercy and warning.

Psalm 51. From Period 3. The Psalmist has been guilty of a great crime and the sense of estrangement from God smites his conscience. As the Psalmist ponders on his misery he learns that its severity is due not only to the actual misdeed itself but to the sinfulness of his heart and that it is this sinfulness which has brought about the feeling of alienation from God. Through his confession he gains comfort from the thought of his forgiveness. There is no longer a temple to receive his public offering but his prayer will nevertheless not be in vain. It does so often happen that from an actual sin we may rise to a higher life.

vv.   1 - 4 This is one of the great penitential psalms. The Psalmist confesses his sin and asks for mercy.
vv.   5 - 8 He pleads the sinfulness of his nature ....
vv.   9 - 12 and prays for the guidance of God's spirit .....
vv. 13 - 17 that he may pay the true sacrifice of praising God.
v. 18 - end He hopes when the Temple is re-built he may be able to repeat his Thanksgiving.

Psalm 52. From Period 2. This is one of the psalms which show the bitterness and feelings of despair over the dissensions which arose from the decline of the Kingdom. One of the conspicuous enemies of the faithful in Jerusalem is denounced by the Psalmist.

vv.   1 - 5 Shows the confidence of the wicked.
vv.   6 - 8 God will overthrow them ......
vv. 9 & 10 while the godly will continue for ever.

DAY TEN

Evening Prayer

Psalm 53. Read notes on Period 3. There is a similarity between this psalm and Psalm 14. The tone is sterner and more vindictive against oppressors of Israel. It may have been written when the Babylonian Empire was about to crumble. God is seen as coming to assess the wickedness of His foes.

vv. 1 - 3   God sees the corruption of the nations....
vv. 4 & 5   and rebukes it from heaven.
vv. 6 & 7   The heathen are confounded and there follows a prayer for the restoration of Israel. (v. 8)

Psalm 54. From Period 2. In the midst of persecution by the heathen the Psalmist finds comfort in the continual worship at the Temple and he sees with the eye of faith the avenging hand of God and just judgement on his persecutors.

vv. 1 - 3   Prayer for help against the enemies.
vv. 4 - 7   The triumph of faith.

Psalm 55. Also from Period 2. This psalm presents a melancholy picture of Jerusalem hastening to its fall - pressure from enemies without - treachery and strife within - all making for insecurity.

vv. 1 - 8   Psalmist prays for help in danger.
vv. 9 - end   Calls on God to punish the wickedness of the city and the treachery of his friend. He finds calm in the thought of God's justice.

DAY ELEVEN

Morning Prayer

Psalm 56. From Period 2. We gather from this psalm that the Psalmist is now captive in a heathen land and his faithfulness to the worship of his country has brought suspicions and persecution. This, however, only serves to deepen his confidence in deliverance by the hand of Jehovah. He foresees the day when Jehovah will overthrow the tyranny of the heathen and establish the religion of Israel over the whole earth.

vv. 1 - 4   In the midst of persecution ....
vv. 5 - 8   the Psalmist trusts in the providence of God.
vv. 9 - end   For He will deliver him in the time of trouble.

Psalm 57. Also from Period 2. The Psalmist hopes for restoration within the Kingdom and he expresses these hopes in poetic terms on behalf of those already in Captivity.

vv. 1 - 6   The Psalmist prays in his affliction ....
vv. 7 - end   and hopes for the restoration of God's Kingdom.

Psalm 58. Also from Period 2. Justice was sacred to eastern nations but this psalm is a bitter outcry against the corruption of the administrators taking upon themselves the title of "gods". However God will ultimately triumph when the whole company of unrighteous judges shall be rooted out.

vv. 1 - 5   The Judges show their real nature by their wicked deeds.
vv. 6 & 7   The Psalmists calls on God to destroy them ....
vv. 8 - end   and foresees their sudden overthrow and the triumph of the righteous.

DAY ELEVEN
Evening Prayer

Psalm 59. This is from Period 2. This psalm written possibly in the time of Josiah the King who may be the author and he is represented in Jerusalem as being invaded by a savage foe; a seething host of horsemen and bowmen surging to and fro. The vivid description of grinning like dogs etc., suggests an eye witness of plundering by day and night.

vv. 1 - 5	He cries to God for help against the fury of the invader.
vv. 6 - 10	He sets forth the threatening danger and the mercy of God.
vv. 11 - 15	He prays to God to let the enemy come back so that they may be slain and be seen by all those in the city.
vv. 16 - 17	Praise of God for deliverance.

Psalm 60. This is from Period 4. This psalm expresses the feeling there was on the return from Captivity; that God would set the people up again because of the disappointment that had followed on the restoration.

vv. 1 - 5	The need for building up the nation again.
vv. 6 - 8	Quotes the victories which had comforted David in his time.
vv. 9 - 12	An assurance to everyone that God would deliver them from their weakness and affliction.

Psalm 61. Read notes on Period 2. The captivity has partially begun and the Psalmist has met the fate of being torn from the Temple but his thoughts are still centred on Jerusalem and the King (possibly Josiah).

vv. 1 - 3	He prays to God from a distant land.
vv. 4 & 5	He longs for the Temple ....,
vv. 6 - 8	and for the safety of the King.

DAY TWELVE

Morning Prayer

Psalm 62. From Period 2. The Psalmist keeps his soul in quietness and confidence in spite of the attempt to drag him away from the worship and the thought of the Almighty which is always with him. A striking resemblance to Elijah who stood alone contending single-handed, without any help or religious sympathy from anyone. We should be filled with admiration at the noble attitude of this author.

vv. 1 - 2   Resignation of the Psalmist to his true faith.
vv. 3 - 7   Amid the attacks of those against him.
vv. 8 - end   These verses show the emptiness of human strength apart from God.

Psalm 63. Also from Period 2. A lamentation in a foreign land by one who longs to return to the Temple. He recalls the happiness and splendour of the services and naturally closes with a prayer for the King whose authority is bound up with those who are faithful to the nation and Temple.

vv. 1 - 7   The Psalmist in exile longs to return to the Temple.
vv. 8 - end   For God has always been his support and shield.

Psalm 64. From Period 2. Enemies are secretly plotting against this Psalmist and he prophesies a certain calamity by which the wicked shall be overthrown and the righteous prevail.

vv. 1 - 4   His prayer for help.
vv. 5 - 7   The plots of the wicked are full of craftiness....
vv. 8 - end   but God shall turn their wickedness against themselves.

DAY TWELVE
Evening Prayer

Psalm 65. From Period 2. We have here a psalm of thanksgiving intended to be sung in the Temple at festivals praising Jehovah the God of nature and the God of history. The dispersion of the Jews was already beginning and this gave the inhabitants of Jerusalem a keener sense of the beauty of the Temple.
vv. 1 - 4 Worthy is God to be praised......
vv. 5 - 8 in the works of nature and His dealings with people.
vv. 9 - 14 Also for the gracious rain which He has sent on the land.

Psalm 66. This psalm is in two parts - quite distinct in mood and subject.
vv. 1 - 11 Seem to be living over again the times of great deliverance under Moses designed as a national thanksgiving.
vv. 12 - 18 Seems to be celebrating the deliverance of an individual intended to be sung in the Temple.

Psalm 67. This comes from Period 4. It looks far beyond the limits of Judah and the immediate prosperity of the Hebrew nation. This psalm breathes a new relationship with the heathen world and with all nations of the earth.
vv. 1 - 4 A prayer that the rule of the God of Israel ....
vv. 5 - 7 may be extended over all nations.

DAY THIRTEEN
Morning Prayer

Psalm 68. From Period 4. This psalm describes the second Dedication of the Temple with grand and elaborate words as the children of the Captivity rejoice to know that Jehovah was again their God and it is He who has brought them home.

vv. 1 - 6   Praise for God's deliverance from the exile in Babylon.
vv. 7 - 10 As the people were led by Moses out of Egypt .....
vv. 11 - 14 and slew kings for their sake.
vv. 15 - 18 Sion had been chosen for God's dwelling and he has mounted it in triumph.
vv. 19 - 23 God has powerfully delivered His chosen people from death and will destroy their enemies.
vv. 24 - 27 The psalm continues with the priest's description of the grand procession to the Temple.
vv. 28 - 31 Kings will come to pay homage to Jehovah.
vv. 32 - end Though Jehovah is King in Heaven, yet His earthly throne is in Sion.

DAY THIRTEEN

Evening Prayer

Psalm 69. Read notes in Period 3. This psalm comes from the earlier times of the captivity when the author was exposed to the scorn heaped on him in his zeal to uphold the religion of his people; but the psalm closes with thoughts of hope in the national restoration.

vv. 1 - 12 Cries for help in persecution and suffering in God's cause.
vv. 13 - 29 Therefore he prays afresh that the enemies may be punished ....
vv. 30 - 37 and the cause of the righteous he hopes shall prevail and prosperity be restored.

Psalm 70. Also from Group 3 and shares the same thoughts as the previous psalm, i.e., the despairing cry of an exile, fierce struggle of a believer's soul and his reviving trust in God.

DAY FOURTEEN
Morning Prayer

Psalm 71. From Period 3. The Psalmist describes here the Captivity; after varied fortunes he is once again threatened by his enemies and gives a noble picture of his training in discipline by putting his calm trust in God, even in old age to face whatever may come to him.

vv. 1 - 8 The Psalmist calls on God to protect him as of old.

vv. 9 - 16 He describes his need, his patience and his gratitude...

vv. 17 - end and speaks of God's righteousness and praises His faithfulness.

Psalm 72. From Period 2. This psalm is a prayer for the King who has just ascended the throne (Josiah possibly) that the Kingdom of David may be fully restored to its former position in the world. It is not to a sword but to a wise and understanding heart that the Psalmist looks for deliverance. Like Solomon, he prays that the King may, by the spirit, be able to discern between good and evil.

vv. 1 - 7 Because the Kingdom has been impoverished, a prayer for the welfare of the King as he begins his reign ..

vv. 8 - 15 and for the greater prosperity of the Kingdom through just administration and protection of the oppressed.

vv. 16 - end That the new King may be a Blessing to everyone through his righteous acts.

DAY FOURTEEN
Evening Prayer

Psalm 73. This psalm comes from Period 3. The faithful Israelites became more and more depressed as the Captivity was prolonged, yet there were lessons to be learnt

		and God would in the end deliver them again as he had delivered them from Egypt.

vv. 1 - 9   The Psalmist is puzzled by the prosperity of the wicked, and..

vv. 10 - 13   that the faithful are drawn after them .....

vv. 14 - 21   until the time comes when his eyes are opened to see as God sees.

vv. 22 - 27   Declares his unchanged trust in God. Is there perhaps here a hint of hope for a life beyond death with God?

Psalm 74. Notes on Period 4. This psalm shows a perplexity that after so much restoration of the Holy City, disaster should come upon the people. Zerubbabel, the Prince, and Joshua, High Priest had not only built the walls up again but united the people. Now there are the miseries of war and destruction.

vv. 1 - 9   Complaints of present evil, and desolation of the Sanctuary.

vv. 10 - 17   Story of former blessings.

vv. 19 to end   Profession of faith and cry to God for help.

DAY FIFTEEN

Morning Prayer

Psalm 75. From Period 2. This psalm speaks of the conviction that the Jews were a favoured people and had been chosen by God and so in the dark days this belief burned brighter than ever. They looked to future prosperity by the light of this assurance which raised them above any present persecution.

vv. 1 - 4   God as the judge of the world....

vv. 5 - 10   and to Him alone does judgement belong. The word "horn" expresses honour or strength.

vv. 11 & 12   God judges people righteously.

Psalm 76. From Period 2. This psalm is written in the calm which followed the victory over the Assyrians and there are signs that a wider vision of the nation of Israel has come as a result, when all the nations will unite together in the acknowledgement and worship of the true God.

vv. 1 - 6   A look at the battlefield showing the mighty works of the Lord against the enemies of Israel.

vv. 7 - end   Righteous judgements of the Lord on the nations of the earth.

Psalm 77. Period 3. The Psalmist lays his life before us in this psalm; in his struggle in a single night with despair on the one hand and hope on the other. If God is still ruling, even with His people in Captivity, then all will be well and he is carried away into a song of triumph becoming a new man.

vv. 1 - 9   The Psalmist shows his great despair in exile.

vv. 10 - 12   Now he thinks of God and His mighty works of old and ......

vv. 13 - end   as a result breaks into a hymn of praise for the nation's deliverance at the Red Sea.

DAY FIFTEEN

Evening Prayer

Psalm 78. This psalm is from Period 4 and the Psalmist calls the people to listen to the lessons of their past history. One of the great teaching psalms of the Jewish nation. Reminds the people that the fulfilment of the promises of God depend on willing co-operation with God. Their history is a rich source of hope, yet warnings and encouragement are needed in the national dark days. Great opportunity in this long psalm for numerous changes of the singing chants, expressing the various moods and moral judgements.

DAY SIXTEEN

Morning Prayer

Psalm 79. From the end of Period 3. At the time of the composition of this psalm there was more than ordinary trouble, even deep distress. The house of David had suffered personal ill-treatment and likewise the city and nation. The whole nation is oppressed by their enemies and the tone of the psalm is full of bitterness called forth by the sufferings of the people and their apparent desertion by God.

vv. 1 - 5   The Psalmist shows the desolation of Jerusalem and he ...

vv. 6 - 11   prays for vengeance on the enemies and for deliverance for Israel.

vv. 12 - end   At the end of this psalm he promises thankfulness.

Psalm 80. From Period 4. This psalm begins with a pathetic appeal to the mercy of God who has allowed Israel to suffer and the remainder of the psalm is a recital of God's fostering care bringing his people from Egypt to Palestine and tending them as His tender vine. This figure of the vine was engraved on the memory of the nation through the Prophets.

vv. 1 - 3   An appeal to God ....

vv. 4 - 7   who appears to be grievously afflicting Israel.

vv. 8 - end   And yet He has always dealt so lovingly with them in the past.

Psalm 81. From Period 4. This psalm seems specially intended for the great festivals in the temple, ushered in by the feast of trumpets or the new moon, and which contained the great day of the Atonement. The enthusiasm with which the services of the new temple were performed made it possible to bring home to the nation in the last verses of this psalm, the great truths about the past.

vv. 1 - 5   A call to praise God ...
vv. 6 -11   who brought Israel out of Egypt.
vv. 12 -16 If the nation had been faithful
v. 17   He would never have failed His people.

DAY SIXTEEN
Evening Prayer

Psalm 82. This psalm is from Group 3. The princes and rulers may claim to be gods but their power is ready to crumble away because it is corrupt and selfish.
vv. 1 - 4   God calls the rulers of the world to judgement.
vv. 5 - 8   A deaf ear will bring sentence upon them.

Psalm 83. This psalm is from Period 4. The walls of Jerusalem were rising up again but the people had still to fight against the craftiness of enemies who would destroy their re-building.
vv. 1 - 8   Prayer for protection from the heathen.
vv. 9 - 18   As the enemies of old were overcome so may those of the present perish.

Psalm 84. This psalm is from Period 3 written during the early years of the Babylonian captivity, possibly by the king in prison, and it seems that pilgrimages sometimes took place. A contrast between the royal confinement and the seeming liberty of its people to visit their country.
vv. 1 - 3   In absence longs for the Holy Place.
vv. 4 - 7   How blest are those who dwell there or who face the danger of pilgrimage.
vv. 8 - end The King's final prayer.

Psalm 85. This is from Period 4 and designed for the Temple worship. A beautifully expressed psalm and now appointed for Christmas Eve. Antiphonal psalm

	between Priest and People. Pictures suffering and depression even after the joyous return to the Holy Land, through attacks by neighbouring nations.
vv. 1 - 7	The peoples' part. Thanksgiving for restoration to the Holy Land.
vv. 8 - 13	The Priest's answer. Reveals his vision to the people of the time when they would see God's glory re-established in His land.

DAY SEVENTEEN

Morning Prayer

Psalm 86. From period 5. In times of decadence it is from the history of the past rather than from present feelings that nations derive their enthusiasm. So this psalm is written to encourage the flagging Hebrews in their present troubles.

vv. 1 - 5	Prayer to God, who will help, for He is good ...
vv. 6 - 10	and rules over the nations.
vv. 11 - 13	The Psalmist will always walk in His ways....
vv. 14 - 17	and trust the Lord God especially when he is in danger.

Psalm 87. From Period 4. This psalm states the hopes of the time when Jehovah promised to return and dwell in the midst of Jerusalem. We can almost hear the inspiring sound of the cymbals and trumpets when the foundation-stone of the new Temple would be laid. The Psalmist pours forth his feelings in song as he realises the grand idea of the whole world under one shepherd, servants of Jehovah, whose Kingdom will be established at Mount Zion.

v. 2	The words "are spoken of thee" refer to the Prophets and especially Isaiah.
v. 3	"Rahab" means "the proud one". A poetical name for Egypt.

vv. 4 - 6 "There was he born" means each individual of all the nations shall have the same rights as the Jews, born in Jerusalem. All people shall be counted as citizens of the whole world as one fold under one shepherd on Mount Zion.

Psalm 88. From Period 2. The Israelites looked for the rewards of righteousness in this present world. An early death was always a fatal blow to their religious beliefs and hopes. So this psalm is of bitter anguish at the thought of mortal sickness. He dwells on his sufferings and there is no ray of hope, such as we so often find even in the most despondent of the psalms.

DAY SEVENTEEN
Evening Prayer

Psalm 89. This psalm is from Period 2. At the time of composition there was more than ordinary trouble for the house of David with personal ill-treatment of the present Anointed of Jehovah and the city and nation likewise.
vv. 1 - 5 From the misery of the time, the Psalmist takes refuge in God's promises to David, ...
vv. 6 - 19 and in His past mercies to Israel.
vv. 20 - 36 How God chose David to be His king and promised success to his seed.
vv. 37 - 50 And yet He has plunged that succession into terrible misery.

DAY EIGHTEEN
Morning Prayer

Psalm 90. From Period 2. This has been called the funeral hymn of the world. It expresses the great truth of the frailty of man and the transitory nature of existence. To the worldly man this simply brings despair and the spirit "to eat, drink and be merry for tomorrow we die". To the spiritual man it is the higher truth of the eternity of God. The lesson it teaches is not despair or fatalism but faith and co-operation with God's will.

vv. 1 - 6 God's power and man's weakness.
vv. 7 - 12 It is sin that brings about human weakness.
vv. 13 - end A prayer for the return of God's favour.

Psalm 91. From Period 4. The destruction and restoration of the Temple brought with them great lessons. First it was the idolatry of other gods which brought about the fall of the Temple.

It's restoration naturally re-kindles the faith of religious enthusiasm and confidence in Jehovah. The Psalmist proclaims anew the old words of comfort and beliefs of the Prophets and Psalmists of old and they have now become more of a reality. Upon this calm and unwavering faith of the Psalmist, the realisation of God's presence is beyond all doubt, transfigured with a new and abiding glory.

vv. 1 - 7 The Psalmist declares the safety of all who trust in God.
vv. 8 - end Unwavering faith in God's presence is shown forth in thankfulness and nobleness of language. What a splendid example of true faith and trust in God this psalm is to all Christians.

Psalm 92. Also from Period 4. Another of the psalms from the period of the revival of the Temple worship after the return from the Captivity. Possibly the same author as the previous psalm and Psalm 93.

vv. 1 - 3 The delight in praising the Lord ...
vv. 4 - 7 for it is He who upholds the true in heart ...
vv. 8 - end and will give His blessing on those who visit His sanctuary.

DAY EIGHTEEN
Evening Prayer

Psalm 93. A Period 2 psalm and a triumphant thanksgiving.
vv. 1 - 3 God reigns in heaven,
vv. 4 & 5 Above the raging of the sea.
v. 6 Holy worship.

Psalm 94. From Period 3. Prolonged captivity naturally increased the depression of the Israelites but the Psalmist depicts the struggle between despair and hope.
vv. 1 - 7 A cry for judgement on the oppressor of Israel....
vv. 8 - 15 but warns the people of the foolishness of trying to ignore the eye of God.
vv. 16 - end A remembrance of God's past mercies will bring more faith and trust in Him as it does with the Psalmist.

DAY NINETEEN
Morning Prayer

Psalm 95. From period 4. This psalm is known as the Venite. As this psalm summoned the Jews of old to "fall down and worship in their restored Temple at Jerusalem", so in the Christian church it has been used from earliest times as an invitation to the congregation to worship at Morning Prayer. The psalm stresses the omnipotence of God which brings such joy but also the great need for obedience in listening to His voice.
vv. 1 - 6 Invitation to praise.
vv. 7 - end A warning against unbelief.

Psalm 96. Period 4. This psalm and the one following are the two great general Thanksgivings in the whole of the Psalter - praising God as the deliverer of old, the present ruler, and the judge of the whole world.
vv. 1 - 6   Praise of Jehovah.
vv. 7 - end Looking forward to God's just and righteous government in the world.

Psalm 97. Also from Period 4. Another Thanksgiving psalm but also it shows the two great lessons learnt during the Captivity, i.e. the folly and wickedness of idolatrous worship and the longing for their nation to become the centre of religious life in the world.
vv. 1 - 6   God rules on high and shows His glory in thunder and lightning.
vv. 7 - end It is in devotion to God that the safety of the nation lies.

DAY NINETEEN
Evening Prayer

Psalm 98. From Period 4. Composed for a congregational service to celebrate the restoration of Jerusalem.
vv. 1 - 4   God has delivered His people.
vv. 5 - 7   Let the world rejoice ...
vv. 8 - 10   for He will build a righteous government.

Psalm 99. From the same Period 4, as the previous psalm.
vv. 1 - 3   Jehovah King of Kings.
vv. 4 - 5   He loves justice.
vv. 6 - 9   Reveals Himself to His servants and must be worshipped.

Psalm 100. The same Period 4 as other previous psalms and is known as the Jubilate. Among the psalms of thanksgiving this stands pre-eminent.

vv. 1 - 2   Praise to God for His creation
vv. 3 & 4   And His loving care for the children of men. The word "truth" means fulfilment of promise.

Psalm 101. Back to David's time Period 1. David longs for wisdom which comes from God, to order the King's household and the government of the country in God's ways, but this must begin with his own heart.

vv. 1 - 5   King David must set a good example himself.
vv. 6 - 11   So must also those in the King's household and court be pure and true.

DAY TWENTY
Morning Prayer

Psalm 102. From Period 3. As the Psalmist lingers among the ruins of the City of Jerusalem (Sion), he was led to think of, and meditate on, the contrast between the perishable things around him and the imperishable nature of God.

vv. 1 - 22   A long prayer of the Psalmist's affliction. (Pelican conveys the idea of loneliness and the owl the mother of ruins).
vv. 23 - 28   He is comforted by the thought of the eternity of God.

Psalm 103. From Period 5. The key note of this psalm is the fatherly love and care of God, and we learn to see God from it in all things near and far and in all things great and small.

vv. 1 - 5   Praise due to God for His love to every individual.
vv. 6 - 9   The revelation of God to all mankind.
vv. 10 - 18   God's mercy in forgiving sins and His compassion.
vv. 19 - end   God's sovereignty over the world.

DAY TWENTY
Evening Prayer

Psalm 104. A grand congregational psalm which could have been written at any time. A hymn of praise to God as the Almighty Creator of the world and sustainer of all things; in Him they live and move and have their being.
vv.   1 - 4   The creation of the Heavens ....
vv.   5 - 9   the Earth ....
vv. 10 - 18   the dry land and all that is in it....
vv. 19 - 23   the heavenly bodies....
vv. 24 - 26   the sea and all that is in it.
vv. 27 - 30   God is the source of all life and .....
vv. 31 - 35   the King and Judge of the world.

DAY TWENTY-ONE
Morning Prayer

Psalm 105. Period 5. When this psalm was written the nation's deliverance from foreign domination was only partial. It therefore brought with it the question of greater restoration of the Kingdom. The successful building of the walls of Jerusalem had brought hope for the more complete restoration of the national revival.
vv.   1 -15   Praise of God who has protected His people.
vv. 16 - 22   The story of Joseph.
vv. 23 - 37   Moses in Egypt.
vv. 38 - end God's protection in the wilderness, giving the Israelites the promised land of Canaan on the condition that the nation kept His Covenant.

DAY TWENTY-ONE
Evening Prayer

Psalm 106. This may have been written during Period 4 or 5. Contains an anaylsis of Jewish history and God's dealing with the nation. Lessons have been learnt from the Captivity such as the unity of God, the evil of idolatry and the conviction of God's love for His people, especially the afflicted and oppressed. The main part of this psalm is chanted by a leader, possibly a priest and the response given by the people.

vv. 1 - 3 The Chorus.
vv. 4 - 44 The Priest reciting the history of the past and showing forth the loving mercy of God.
vv. 45 - end Chorus of people and Priest.

DAY TWENTY-TWO
Morning Prayer

Psalm 107. Also from period 5. This psalm shows how the nation has profited by the adversity of the Captivity in Babylon. The people had learned the lessons of the evil of idolatry, conviction of God's fatherly love for all, the value of obedience, and the fact that God's promises depended on national morality.

vv. 1 - 9 Thanksgiving for the re-union of scattered exiles, some of whom had been delivered from wanderings and famine.
vv. 10 - 16 Some had been delivered from prison....
vv. 17 - 22 and from sickness.
vv. 23 - 32 Also many delivered from the perils by sea.
vv. 33 - end In praise of God as Creator and Preserver of His people.

DAY TWENTY-TWO
Evening Prayer

Psalm 108. This psalm is compiled from Psalm 57: vv 8 - 12 and Psalm 60 vv. 5 - 12. It is not easy to place in any period but most probably from David's time - Period 1. The clue to this psalm is to realise that it was not just to maintain the recognition of Jehovah in the Hebrew nation but to win God's acknowledgement in other lands as well.

vv.   1 - 6 David is perplexed by the nation being threatened on all sides and turns to seek the help of Jehovah in carrying out the mission of the Hebrew people.

vv.   7 - end David receives his answer in a prophetic promise of deliverance.

Psalm 109. This psalm reveals the dark picture of Captivity - an outburst of bitterness against the treachery of persecution. It is from Period 3.

vv.   1 - 4 The Psalmist in persecution ....

vv.   5 - 19 prays to God for retribution.

vv. 20 - 28 And to have mercy on him for his unfaithfulness.

vv. 29 & 30 He rejoices in God.

DAY TWENTY-THREE
Morning Prayer

Psalm 110. Period 1. King David is setting out to war after prayer and the prophet is describing Jehovah seated beside the King in his chariot. The God, whose priest he was, would fight beside him. (Melchisedek was a pre-Israelite priest and king of Jerusalem before David captured the city).

vv.   1 - 3 Relates God's promise of help and victory.

vv. 4 - end The sacredness of the King's leadership and the description of the battlefield.

Psalm 111. From Period 5. Praise for the greatness of Jehovah and His works, and of the redemption of the people from foreign domination.

Psalm 112. Also from Period 5. This and the previous Psalm 111, are closely connected in praising the greatness and the goodness of God's worshippers.

Psalm 113. From period 5. This psalm and Psalm 114 most likely form part of a Passover Service and speak of God as the deliverer and upholder at all times. Psalm 113 makes a very good Thanksgiving to say after Holy Communion.

DAY TWENTY-THREE
Evening Prayer

Psalm 114. From the Fifth Period of psalms and praises Jehovah as the Almighty Deliverer, especially from Egypt. Nowhere do we find a grander picture of that Exodus.
vv. 1 & 2 Supports the belief that this psalm was written on the return from Captivity.
vv. 3 - 8 God as the source of all life.

Psalm 115. From Period 4 and sung during the trials and tribulations of the new community during the rebuilding of Jerusalem, concentrating on the need for true religion; the heathen idol worship is mocked by the Psalmist.
vv. 1 - 11 The invisible God of Israel contrasted with the gods of the heathen.
vv. 12 - 15 These verses probably sung by the high priest.
vv. 16 - 18 These verses sung by the people.

DAY TWENTY-FOUR
Morning Prayer

Psalm 116. Period 4. The joy and gratitude called forth by the restoration of the national independence is found here in the Psalmist's private devotion. There is still trouble but he has faith in Jehovah that in the future all will be well.
vv. 1 - 6   Calls on Jehovah for help.
vv. 7 - 13 He has delivered him before and now receives God's blessings with gratitude.
vv.14 - end Praise will then be offered in the restored Temple.

Psalm 117. From Period 5. A short praise of Jehovah.

Psalm 118. Period 2. Everything about this psalm points to an early date - the poetic style, the content etc. It is for a royal victory procession into the Temple after a successful capaign. Note the 'responses' in the final section of Psalm 24.
vv. 1 - 4   Sung by the Choir as the procession approaches the Holy Place.
vv. 5 - 9   Thanksgiving for deliverance from the heathen, led by the Leader of the Choir.
vv. 10 - 12 Leader and Choir alternatively.
vv. 13 - 18 Leader gives thanks for restoration of the people to their country.
vv. 19 - 23 The procession reaches the Holy Place.
vv.24 - 25 Sung by the people.
vv. 26 - 27 The High Priest blesses the procession and the offerings and the sacrifice of the people.
v. 28   Leader of the Choir.
v. 29   Sung by the Choir.

DAYS TWENTY-FOUR, TWENTY-FIVE AND TWENTY-SIX
Evening Prayer

Psalm 119 vv. 1 - 32, vv. 73 - 104 and vv. 145 - 176. The whole of this psalm is from the Period 5. It is the work of one who is able to look back on a faithful life to Jehovah through all the times of persecution and stress and still blest with a sense of God's love and a deep desire to do His will. Psalm 119 is a treasured expression of the high feelings in this period of the nation; religion is no longer connected with national triumphs but there is now a wide gulf between the godly and the world. There is a longing for a fuller knowledge of God's law. The repeated prayer is for God's guidance to give the Psalmist new life.

DAYS TWENTY-FIVE AND TWENTY-SIX
Morning Prayer

Psalm 119. vv 33-77, vv 105-144. The whole of this psalm comes from Period 5 and notes can be found under the twenty-fourth evening.

DAY TWENTY-SEVEN
Morning Prayer

Psalm 120. Period 3. The psalmist pictures the pilgrim going through the desert from Babylon and his captivity there to his home in Palestine, beset on his way by hostile tribes who have no respect for the obligations of a treaty. It appears that this psalm is the first of fifteen which end with Psalm 134 and form a small collection by themselves, a group sung as "going up" from Captivity to Jerusalem.

Psalm 121. Period 3. The exiled pilgrim on his way home from Babylon longs to see the hills of his own country and he overcomes doubt with trust and inward conflicts with peace. This particular psalm speaks of the dangers of the desert, burning sun by day and perils from lawless tribes by night.

vv. 1 - 4   The yearning for help.
vv. 5 - 8   The assurance that God watches over his journey. This psalm is sometimes used for anyone who is about to go on a journey and could be called the Traveller's Psalm.

Psalm 122. Period 4. This psalm suggests a blessing on a party of pilgrims, written possibly by an ageing exile, not able to make the journey himself across the desert. The departure of his friends reminds him of the time when he too had responded (v. 8) and he pours forth the praises of Jerusalem as the keystone of national unity.

v. 1   The exile.
vv. 2 - 5   In remembrance of former pilgrimage.
vv. 6 - 9   He bids "Godspeed" to his nation.

Psalm 123. Period 3. The exiles, in patient longing for the summons to return to their own land.

v. 2   Suggests that they are slaves waiting for their master's hand to beckon them and in verse 4 "wealthy" may more exactly mean "those that are at ease".

Psalm 124. Period 4. This psalm suggests that the nation of Israel in Captivity had been almost entirely swallowed up by the great numbers of their oppressors. The Psalmist's faith had been sorely tried by the mockery of the heathen but the day dawned at last and the captives were set free.

vv. 1 - 4   A thanksgiving.
vv. 5 - end   For deliverance from Captivity.

Psalm 125.   Period 4. A new community had already been established in Jerusalem but the building of the Temple was at a standstill from inroads made by hostile tribes. After the first joy of the return from Captivity, a reaction had set in and it appears from this psalm and Psalm 126 that there was internal dissension but the writer dispels the fears of the despairing by his confident assurance of coming recovery.

DAY TWENTY-SEVEN
Evening Prayer

Psalm 126. From Period 4. A contrast between the dangers of the present and the great joy of the first years after the return from Captivity.
vv. 1 - 4   A remembrance of the joys of the return from Captivity.
vv. 5 - end   A prayer for help in present difficulties.

Psalm 127. From Period 4 and spoken to those who have experienced the great deliverance.
vv. 1 - 3   Need to remember God's blessing on all their work and rebuilding.
vv. 4   Young people as the strength in the city, defending its walls.

Psalm 128. Like the previous psalms it is from Period 4 and is a similar hope that the new Jerusalem may be made safe for its people.

vv.1 - end   That the new families may be blessed.
vv. 1 - 8   God has saved Israel from the hand of the oppressor.

Psalm 129. Also from Period 4 and is an outburst of joy at deliverence from Captivity.
vv. 1 - 8   God has saved Israel from the hand of the oppressor.

Psalm 130. This is from Period 3 and bemoans the sufferings of the Psalmist's brethren as he longs for the release from Captivity.

Psalm 131. Also from Period 3. The Psalmist has learnt from adversity to wait patiently and submissively for the blessings which are sure to come eventually.

DAY TWENTY-EIGHT
Morning Prayer

Psalm 132. Period 4. The Psalmist here is full of the memory of David and his city Zion and offers a prayer to God to remember His promises and once more to honour His chosen dwelling-place amid the present misery and ruin. It is only in the rebuilding of the Temple and the renewal of worship that the Psalmist will see the return of God's favour and His holy resting-place.
vv. 1 - 7   God's promise to David is now fulfilled for the Temple.
vv. 8 - 12   The Psalmist prays that Jehovah will come to His Temple again.
vv. 13 - end   Zion is the seat of Jehovah where David's seed shall never cease to reign.

Psalm 133. Period 4. Other psalms such as 127 and 128 have the thought that the Israelites now restored to their fatherland look upon their children born, not to exile, but to be a source of strength to the Lord's people. But here the poet has the thought not just of a united family but of a united nation. The blessing of national unity.

Psalm 134. Period 4. A temple evening hymn in which the Psalmist exhorts the Priests and Levites to the devotional performance of their duties.

v. 4   Is the answer of the Priests.

Psalm 135. Period 5. A song of praise. This is the often repeated cry of the Psalmist that Jehovah is the mighty worker, creator of the universe and who has defeated the gods of the heathen.

vv. 1 - 7   The greatness of God in creation.
vv. 8 - 14   The protection of His people.
vv. 15 - end God compared with the vanity of idols.

DAY TWENTY-EIGHT

Evening Prayer

Psalm 136. From Period 5. Thoughts of Psalm 135 here appear in a different arrangement as a song of praise following the return from Captivity.

Psalm 137. From Period 4. Recalls the sorrows of the exile and the love of their mother city.

vv. 7 - 9   This shows that the Hebrews had not learnt the lesson of mercy and forgiveness of their enemies but rather cry still for vengeance and a curse on them.

Psalm 138. Also from Period 4. Once, the hopes of the Jews were the destruction and subjection of the heathen, now the prayer is that nations may be converted to the worship of Jehovah.

vv. 1 -3   Praise of God for his truth.
vv. 4 - 6   May the Princes of the heathen be converted to Him.
vv. 7 & 8   That God may complete his work.

DAY TWENTY-NINE
Morning Prayer

Psalm 139. Period 4. The Psalmist brings out two important truths; the mysterious connection of the spirit of man with the spirit of God, and secondly, the insignificance of man and his dependence on God as Creator, upholder and ever-present friend. We can compare the words of David in Psalm 8 (verse 4 and 5). The experience of three centuries of affliction since Period 1 (David's time) such as no nation had yet undergone and survived, these two truths had become even more firmly fixed in their belief.

vv. 1 - 5   God knows everything.
vv. 6 - 11   God is everywhere.
vv.12 - 18   God is merciful.
vv.19-end   Will God punish the wicked? Not so much for Israel's vengeance but for God's own honour. The Psalmist did not live to see the more gentle influence towards Israel's enemies of later years.

Psalm 140. Period 2. Psalms 140, 141 and 142 apparently belong to the period after the Assyrian invasion and the country is split between the followers of Jehovah and the heathen. Threats and violence are used to win over the faithful to give up their worship of Jehovah. The similarity of the language point to one author of these three psalms and he is man of position but we see him overcoming the maliciousness, treachery and slander through his faith, even unshaken by imprisonment (Psalm 142 v.9).

vv. 1 - 3   A prayer for deliverance from malicious attacks.
vv. 4 - 5   The snares of the ungodly.
vv 6 - 8   The Psalmist's hope is in Jehovah.
vv.9 - end   He will avenge the cause of the patient and upright.
Psalm 141. Period 2. The violent persecution of the worshippers of Jehovah is still present and attempts are made to

		persuade the Psalmist to join the unbelievers by letting his voice be heard in high places.
vv.	1 & 2	The Psalmist prays to God at eventide .....
vv.	3 & 4	... for strength to resist the wicked .... and that his voice may not be heard at their festivities, for he trusts in God for deliverance.

DAY TWENTY-NINE
Evening Prayer

Psalm 142. This is from the Second Period of psalms, and probably the period following the invasion by the Assyrians. The court in Jerusalem had become corrupt so the Psalmist prays for deliverance from the temptation to go along with the degeneracy.

vv.	1 - 6	Jehovah is the only helper in his distress.
vv.	7 - 9	The righteous will look on His deliverance as a sign of good over evil.

Psalm 143. Taken from Period 5. Although the return has taken place and the exile forgotten, there was much to be done in re-building the national life. There were still the enemies of the Jewish religion and was much opposition in the nation.

vv.	1 - 4	Prayer to God in time of suffering.
vv.	5 - 9	Remembering His doings of old, and ....
vv.	10 - 12	trust that God will hear his prayer.

DAY THIRTY
Morning Prayer

Psalm 144. This psalm must be divided into two parts: the first eleven verses, apparently selected for its warlike spirit, and is from Period 1; and the second half symbolises the time of peace and prosperity in Period 5.

vv. 1 - 4   The praise of God
vv. 5 - 8   A prayer for deliverance ....
vv. 9 - 11   as He delivered David.
vv. 12 - 15   Picture of people living in the happy contentment of pastoral life is the final hope of the Psalmist.

Psalm 145. Period 5. This is one of the group of psalms towards the end of the Psalter showing the revival of national life. The successful rebuilding of the City and restoration of the old ritualistic worship seemed to herald.

Psalm 146. Period 5. In this psalm we are taken back to the thoughts in Psalm 103 of the paternal affection of God for His people. In the former days of national prosperity, the mighty and the exalted had alone seemed worthy, but now the whole nation through suffering had reached the sense of God's fatherly love. The power of kings and princes is as nothing to him whose help is in the Lord his God.

vv. 1 - 3   The weakness of kings.
vv. 4 - 6   The greatness of faith.
vv 7 - end   The goodness of God.

DAY THIRTY

Evening Prayer

All four psalms forming the conclusion of the Psalter are from Period 5.

Psalm 147. Psalm in praise of God for a preservation of Israel and the complete restoration of Jerusalem.

vv. 1 - 11   Praise for rebuilding the city and for creating and maintaining the universe.
vv. 12 - 20   Praise for return to prosperity.

Psalm 148. The praise of the Creator due from heaven and earth and from His people.

Psalm 149. A song of victory due to the awakening enthusiasm on the return from exile, but their minds still closed to the idea of God not only as a saviour but also of mercy to enemies - a wider lesson that the people should have learnt from foreign nations during the Captivity.

vv. 7 - 9 Spirit of exclusion and merciless extermination thought necessary for their enemies at an earlier period should now by this time have become distasteful and wrong.

Psalm 150. A kind of "Gloria", full of thanksgiving.

Psalm 66
"Juilate Deo, omnis terra".
"O be joyful in God, all ye lands".

51

The Psalms

Some key-quotations

'None of these kinds of prayer is to be neglected by those who are resolved diligently to live for the glory of God and of His Christ. And I am of the opinion that diversity and variety in the prayers and psalms of the appointed hours are useful, and for this reason, that a want of variety often reduces slothfulness of mind, so that it becomes inattentive, while by changing and varying the psalms and the reading at each office our fervour may be rekindled, and our attention renewed.'
(Basil of Caesarea)

'How did I weep in thy hymns and canticles, touched to the quick by the voices of thy sweet-tuned church! The voices flowed into mine ears and the Truth distilled into my heart, whence the affections of my devotion overflowed, and tears ran down, and happy was I therein.'
(Augustine)

'Some of the clergy spend their time not in offering to God the sacrifice of praise, but rather in gabbling through the service, with frequent interruptions of vain and unprofitable discourse and unlawful murmurs to each other.'
(John de Grandisson - Bishop of Exeter 1327 - 1369).

'See that what you sing with your mouth, you believe in your heart, and what you believe in your heart, you prove with works.' *(Statuta Ecclesiae Antiquae)*

'..... it is a marvel that the Psalter, the product of a small, much despised, often persecuted, always exclusive people, should have been adopted, not under any pressure, but simply by reason of its sheer merit, by every branch of the Christian church.' *(John Lamb - formerly Presbyterian Doctor of Theology)*

'The psalm-tones have a noble fluency, and impersonal dignity and an impressive beauty.' *(John Lamb)*

'One of the effects of using such religious poetry as the vehicle of our own faith and of our own uncertainty is to give us a wider context for where we stand.' *(Peter Ackroyd - from his book on the Psalms - now Professor Emeritus of Old Testament Theology at King's College, London).*